Nora the Naturalist's Animals

Rock Pool Animals

W

FRANKLIN WATTS

LONDON•SYDNEY

Franklin Watts
First published in Great Britain in 2015 by The Watts Publishing Group

Designed and illustrated by David West

Dewey number 577.699
HB ISBN 978 1 4451 4497 9

Printed in Malaysia

Franklin Watts
An imprint of
Hachette Children's Group
Part of The Watts Publishing Group
Carmelite House
50 Victoria Embankment
London EC4Y 0DZ

An Hachette UK Company
www.hachette.co.uk

www.franklinwatts.co.uk

NORA THE NATURALIST'S ANIMALS ROCK POOL ANIMALS
was produced for Franklin Watts by
David West Children's Books, 6 Princeton Court, 55 Felsham Road, London SW15 1AZ

Nora the Naturalist says:
I will tell you something
more about the animal.

Learn what this
animal eats.

Where in the
world is the
animal found?

Its size is revealed!

What animal group
is it – mammal, bird,
reptile, amphibian,
insect, or something
else?

Interesting facts.

Contents

Nora the Naturalist says:
Crabs have an outer layer of armoured shell, called an exoskeleton. Many crabs walk sideways.

Crabs

You may find crabs hidden amongst the seaweed in rock pools. They are known for their powerful pincer claws.

Edible crab

Crabs feed on any food available, such as **molluscs**, worms, other crustaceans and plant matter.

Crabs can be found in the oceans and on seashores all over the world.

Adult crabs may have a body width of up to 25 centimetres and weigh as much as 3 kilogrammes.

Crabs are members of the **crustacean** family.

Many types of crab, like this brown crab (also known as the edible crab), are delicious to eat.

5

Lobsters

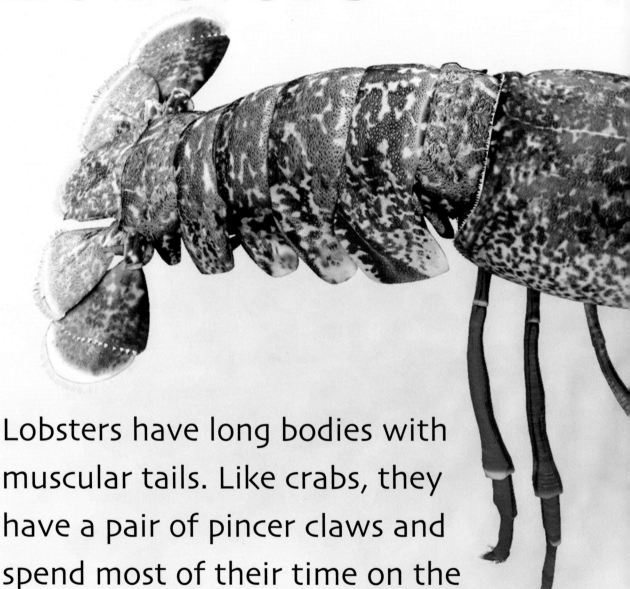

Lobsters have long bodies with muscular tails. Like crabs, they have a pair of pincer claws and spend most of their time on the sea floor, in crevices and burrows.

Lobsters typically eat live **prey**, such as fish, molluscs, other crustaceans, worms and some plant life.

Lobsters are found in all oceans.

Generally lobsters are between 25–50 centimetres in length.

Lobsters are members of the crustacean family.

Lobsters move by slowly walking on the sea floor. To escape a **predator** they swim backwards quickly by curling and uncurling their tail at speeds of up to 5 metres per second.

Nora the Naturalist says: Like crabs, lobsters must moult in order to grow. This means they shed their outer shell and wait a few hours until the new one hardens.

Blue lobster

Small shrimps will eat **plankton**. As they grow larger, they scavenge on dead sea animals that have fallen to the sea floor.

Shrimps are found in all the oceans of the world.

Shrimps are about 2 centimetres long but some shrimps (often called prawns) grow to over 25 centimetres.

Shrimps are members of the crustacean family.

The tails of shrimps can be delicious to eat. They are caught around the world and are also farmed for us to eat.

Shrimp

8

Shrimps

Shrimps are one of the most common sea animals to be found in rock pools. These tiny crustaceans can be quite difficult to find as they often have see-through bodies.

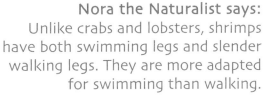

Nora the Naturalist says:
Unlike crabs and lobsters, shrimps have both swimming legs and slender walking legs. They are more adapted for swimming than walking.

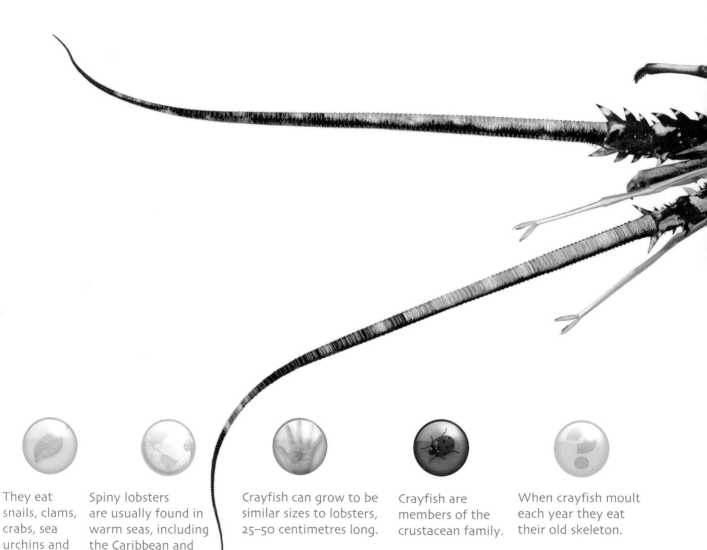

They eat snails, clams, crabs, sea urchins and dead sea animals.

Spiny lobsters are usually found in warm seas, including the Caribbean and the Mediterranean, and in Australasia and South Africa.

Crayfish can grow to be similar sizes to lobsters, 25–50 centimetres long.

Crayfish are members of the crustacean family.

When crayfish moult each year they eat their old skeleton.

Crayfish

Crayfish

Although sometimes called spiny lobsters, or crawfish, these crustaceans are different from lobsters. They may be found near the shore, hiding under rocks.

Fish

All sorts of fish can be found in rock pools. Some are **juveniles** that will eventually leave for the ocean. Others are resident, shoreline fish, such as blennies and gobies.

Rock-pool blenny

Nora the Naturalist says:
Some rock pool fish, such as rockfish, have sharp spines in the fins on their backs. In some species these can be venomous.

12

Most rock pool fish feed on small crustaceans, although some larger species eat other fish as well.

The types of rock pool fish vary, depending on the ocean they live in.

Most rock pool fish are between 10–30 centimetres in length.

These fish are members of the ray-finned fishes. This means their fins are webs of skin with bony spines.

There are many rock pool fish, some of which have strange names such as butterfish, lumpsucker and worm pipefish!

Rock goby

Rockfish

13

Starfish

Starfish are among the most well-known sea animals found on the seabed. They usually have five arms, although some species have many more. They have many tubed feet that run along the underside of the arms.

Underside view of starfish

Starfish are found in all oceans around the world.

Starfish feed on animals living on the sea floor, such as clams, oysters, small fish and sea snails. They may also eat **algae** and other plant matter.

Starfish grow to between 12–24 centimetres in length.

Starfish belong to the family called **echinoderms**, which includes sea urchins, sand dollars and sea cucumbers.

Starfish have a mouth on their underside, in the centre. Some species can live up to 34 years.

Top view of starfish

Nora the Naturalist says: There are around 1,600 different types of starfish. Some have the ability to regrow lost arms.

15

Jellyfish

Watch out for these sea creatures. They have dangerous stinging tentacles. They are often found washed up on beaches and in rock pools after storms.

Black sea nettle

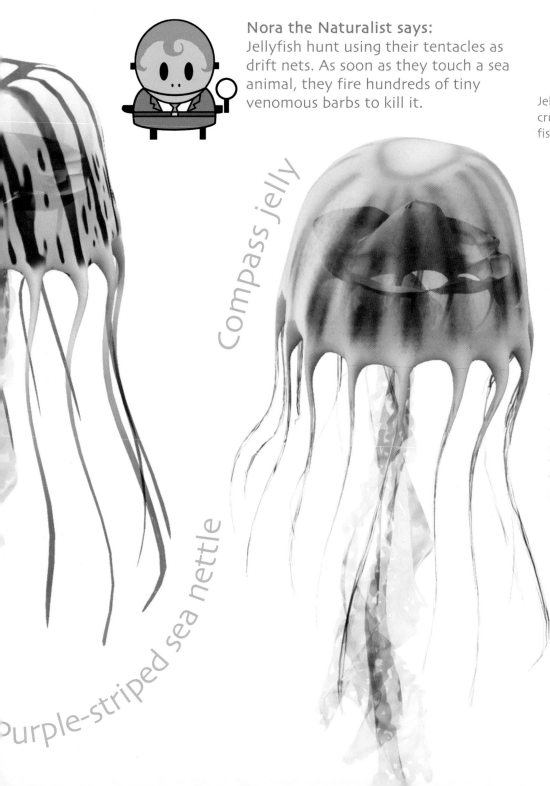

Nora the Naturalist says:
Jellyfish hunt using their tentacles as drift nets. As soon as they touch a sea animal, they fire hundreds of tiny venomous barbs to kill it.

Compass jelly

Purple-striped sea nettle

Jellyfish feed on plankton, crustaceans, fish eggs, small fish and other jellyfish.

Jellyfish are found in every ocean, from the surface to the deep sea. A few jellyfish live in freshwater.

The smallest jellyfish have bell discs less than 1.6 millimetres in diameter, with short tentacles which they trawl around on the bottoms of rocky pools.

Jellyfish are creatures of the **cnidaria** family.

A group of jellyfish is called a bloom.

Octopus eat small fish, shrimps, crab, lobsters, scallops, mussels and clams.

 Octopus are found in all the world's oceans.

 The giant Pacific octopus can grow to an armspan of 4.3 metres. One of the smallest species is the California Lilliput octopus, which measures less than 2.5 centimetres across.

 Octopus are members of the **cephalopod** family that includes squid and cuttlefish.

 Octopus are masters of disguise. They can change the colour of their skin as well as its texture to look like crumbly rock or spiky seaweed.

Octopus

Octopus are very intelligent sea creatures. They have eight arms and no bones, which allows them to squeeze through the smallest of gaps. If they are attacked they squirt out thick, blackish ink in a large cloud.

Nora the Naturalist says:
An octopus can squirt out jets of water to help it escape from predators.

Octopus

19

Nora the Naturalist says:
Take care not to step on a sea urchin. The sharp spines can be very painful.

Sea urchins

Sea Urchins

Sea urchins are small, spiny, ball-like animals. They have tube feet, similar to those of a starfish. Their long, sharp spines protect them from predators.

Sea urchin shell

Sea urchins feed mostly on algae, but can also feed on sea cucumbers and other slow-moving sea creatures.

Sea urchins are found in all the oceans around the world.

Sea urchins typically measure from 6–12 centimetres across. The largest can grow up to 36 centimetres.

Sea urchins belong to the family called echinoderms, which includes starfish, sand dollars and sea cucumbers.

Sea urchins' teeth are self-sharpening and can chew through stone.

Some sea creatures that live in shellls, such as clams, eat plankton. Others, such as sea snails, eat small molluscs.

Nautilus are cephalopods with tentacles like a squid. They live in the deep oceans and only their shells end up in the shallows.

These shelled sea creatures are members of the mollusc family.

Most of these molluscs grow to between the size of a finger nail to the size of a hand. Some, such as the giant clam, can measure as much as 120 centimetres across.

Sea molluscs are found in oceans all over the world.

Horn shells

Sea snails

Clam

Whelks

Seashells

Many rock pools and beaches contain a variety of seashells. They are the the remains of different types of sea creatures from sea snails to scallops and clams.

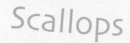

Nautilus

Scallops

Nora the Naturalist says:
Curly shells, such as horn shells and whelks, are sea snails. Scallops and clams live in a shell with two hinged parts. They are called bivalves.

Glossary

algae
Small, simple organisms.

cephalopod
Member of the mollusc family, with a large head, eyes and tentacles.

cnidaria
Simple animals with stinging cells.

crustaceans
Mainly water animals with a hard outer skeleton.

echinoderms
Sea creatures that include starfish and sea urchins.

juvenile
A young animal.

molluscs
The family of animals that includes squid, cuttlefish, octopus and snails.

plankton
Microscopic organisms that live in water.

predator
An animal that hunts other animals for food.

prey
An animal that is hunted for food.

Index

24